MAKING
PRESENTS

• JULIET BAWDEN •

HAMLYN

HANDY HINTS

For some of the presents you are going to make in this book, you may need to use a hot oven, special kinds of glue and varnish, a sharp knife and a pair scissors. Be very careful when you are using them and always make sure that an adult is there to help you.

Wear an apron or old shirt when you are making something a bit messy. Before you start to make anything, cover your work table with sheets of old newspaper or a plastic cloth.

ACKNOWLEDGEMENTS

Presents made by Karen Radford,
Ann Marie Mulligan and Anne Sharples
Photographs by David Johnson
Illustrations by Elizabeth Kerr

HAMLYN CHILDREN'S BOOKS
Series Editor : Anne Civardi
Series Designer : Anne Sharples
Production Controller : Linda Spillane

Published in 1993 by
Hamlyn Children's Books
Part of Reed International Books,
Michelin House, 81 Fulham Road, London SW3 6RB

ISBN 0 600 57552 7

Books printed and bound by Proost, Belgium

CONTENTS

MATERIALS, TIPS AND HINTS

In this book there are all sorts of easy but exciting presents for you to make. There are presents for babies, brothers and sisters, friends, mums, dads and grandparents.

You can probably find many of the things you need to make them with around the house, but you may need to buy a few special things.

Before you start making a present, read the instructions carefully to find out what you need. The handy hints give you lots of extra ideas and help you to make the presents really well.

Things to collect

Cardboard boxes and plastic cartons, such as yoghurt pots, cheese cartons, margarine or butter cartons.

Cardboard tubes, sweet tubes, egg cartons, tin foil and tomato paste tubes.

Card - empty cereal boxes are strong and can easily be cut with scissors. The backs of notepads are also useful.

Paper - old newspapers, scraps of coloured paper, used stamps, drawing paper, old magazines, old wrapping paper, birthday cards and old postcards.

Used lollipop sticks, ice lolly sticks, garden canes or thin straight sticks.

String, ribbon, wool, corks plasticine, bag ties, paper clips, buttons and beads.

Useful tips

1. You will need poster paints or water colour paints for some of the presents you make. Ready-mixed poster paints are sold in pots. For a few projects you will need acrylic or enamel paints.

Before you varnish a present, make sure you have the right varnish. Some are oil-based, some water-based. You can also use clear nail varnish.

Put lids back tightly on glues and paints to stop them from drying out.

Wash your paintbrushes well after you have used them and store them with the bristles facing upwards. Remember to wash oil-based varnish and oil paintbrushes in white spirit.

Keep modelling materials, such as self-hardening clay or salt-dough, in plastic bags to stop them from drying out. Keep salt-dough in the fridge.

Sometimes you can make a present with more than one material. Instead of salt-dough you could use self-hardening clay or papier mâché.

2. There are different makes of self-hardening clay. Read the instructions on the packet very carefully to see how long they take to harden in the oven. Some do not need to be baked at all.

3. You can make papier mâché with either wallpaper paste and water or PVA (polyvinyl acetate) glue mixed with water. The PVA mixture will dry the fastest. Or you can just use flour and water.

4. To make many of the presents you need glue. Glue sticks are clean and easy to use. Strong glue, such as UHU, works well on rubber, cardboard and paper. Copydex is best for fabrics.

NIFTY NAME PLATES

You can make these colourful name plates very easily out of salt, flour and water. Here are lots of ideas on how to decorate and paint them, and the different shapes and sizes you can make.

Things you need

300g salt, 300g plain flour and 1 tbs of oil
Water, a baking tray and baking paper
Water colour paints and paintbrushes
Water-based varnish and some paper clips

A nifty name plate

Making the dough

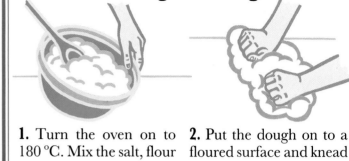

1. Turn the oven on to 180 °C. Mix the salt, flour and oil together in a bowl. Mix in the water, a little at a time, until you have a big ball of dough.

2. Put the dough on to a floured surface and knead it with your hands until it is very smooth and elastic. If it is too dry, add a little more water.

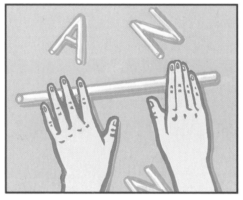

1. Draw the shape of your name plate on to some baking paper. Sprinkle the paper with flour and then press a lump of dough on to the paper to fill the shape.

2. To make the letters on your name plate, roll out some thin sausage shapes of dough. Shape each of the sausage shapes into the letters of your name.

3. Carefully press the letters on to your name plate and add some decorations. Then push a paper clip into the top, as shown, so that you can hang it up later on.

4. Put the name plate and baking paper on to a baking tray and bake it in the middle of the oven until it is hard. This should take about 1½ hours.

5. Take the name plate out of the oven and wait until it is completely cool. Then paint it with bright water colour or poster paints. Let the paint dry.

6. Varnish the name plate on the front and let it dry. Then varnish the back. When it is dry, brush another coat on to the front and back. Leave it to dry.

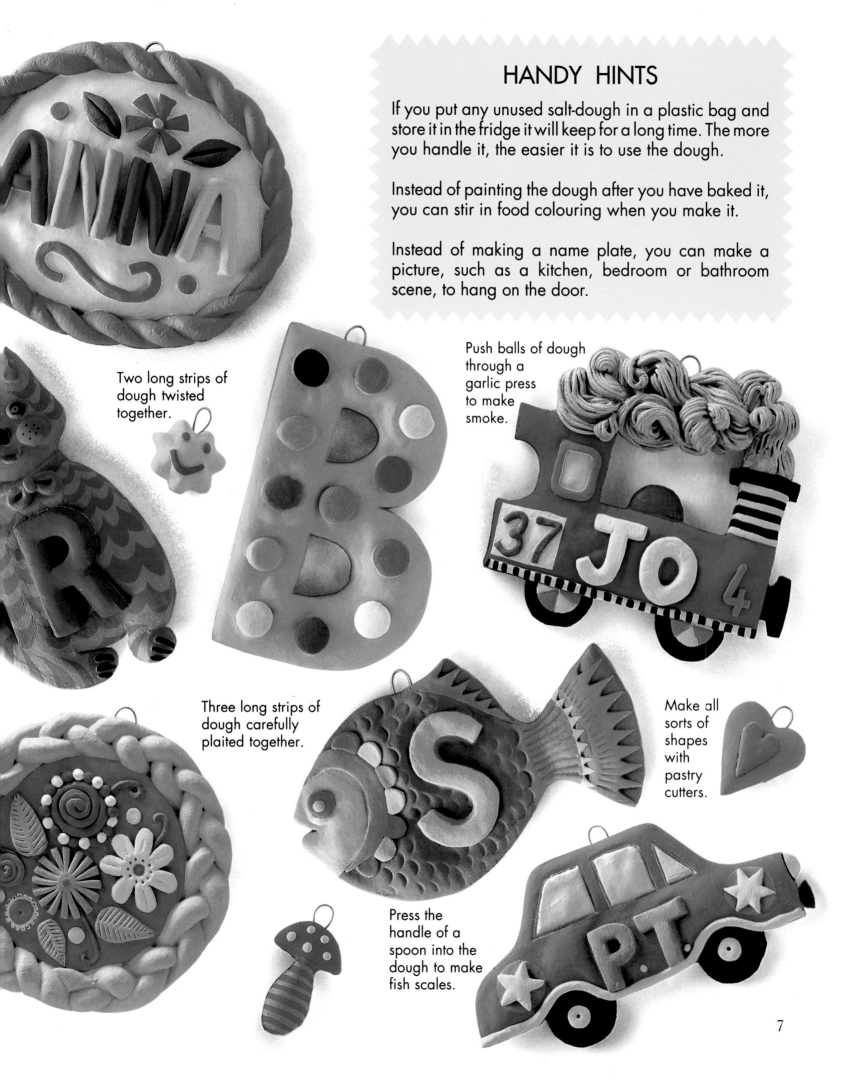

If you put any unused salt-dough in a plastic bag and store it in the fridge it will keep for a long time. The more you handle it, the easier it is to use the dough.

Instead of painting the dough after you have baked it, you can stir in food colouring when you make it.

Instead of making a name plate, you can make a picture, such as a kitchen, bedroom or bathroom scene, to hang on the door.

Two long strips of dough twisted together.

Push balls of dough through a garlic press to make smoke.

Three long strips of dough carefully plaited together.

Make all sorts of shapes with pastry cutters.

Press the handle of a spoon into the dough to make fish scales.

PERKY PINK PIGGY BANK

For a really useful present, you can make this special pink piggy bank. It is made out of papier mâché (layers of newspaper and glue) shaped around a round balloon. You can also use different shaped balloons to make other animals, such as a crocodile or a fish. They will take a couple of days to make as each layer of papier mâché takes a while to dry.

Things you need for the pink pig

A small round balloon
Newspaper
Wallpaper paste or PVA glue
  and water
Five corks and a pin
Masking tape
Strips of thin card
Scissors
Thin wire (a dustbin bag tie is ideal)
Water or poster paints
A paintbrush

Perky
pink
pig

Making the pig

 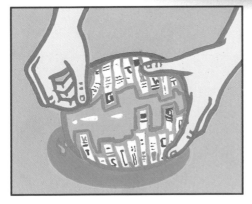 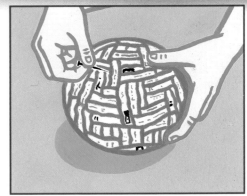

1. Blow up the balloon to the size you want the pig to be. Tie a knot in it. Mix the wallpaper paste following the instructions on the packet. Then tear the sheets of newspaper into strips about 2 cm wide and 7 cm long.

2. Cover a strip of paper with paste, wiping off the extra paste between your thumb and first finger. Stick the paper on to the balloon. Do the same with more strips of paper until the balloon is covered. Leave it to dry.

3. Stick six layers of paper on to the balloon, leaving each one to dry before adding the next. When they are all dry, carefully stick a pin through the papier mâché shell so that you burst the round balloon inside it.

Fantastic fish
money box

HANDY HINTS

You can make your own paste from one cup of flour and three cups of water. Mix the flour with a little of the water in a saucepan, stirring until it becomes a smooth paste. Add the rest of the water and stir. Ask a grown-up to heat the mixture until it boils, stirring all the time. Simmer until the paste thickens. Let the mixture cool.

Instead of using wallpaper paste, you can use PVA glue mixed with three times as much water. This dries very fast and gives a smooth finish.

Paint the pig with clear varnish or watered down PVA glue to give it a hard, strong finish.

Shape this crazy crocodile around a long, thin balloon. Add a card nose and tail, and cork feet.

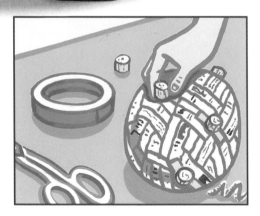

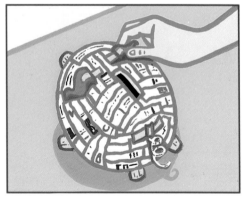

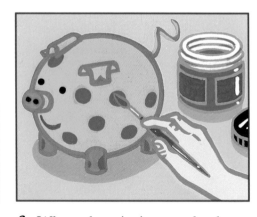

4. Cut one cork in half and tape it on to the papier mâché shell to make the pig's nose. Tape on the other four corks to make the legs. Shape the wire into a curly tail and cover it with papier mâché. Tape it on to the body.

5. Cut out two cardboard ears and tape them on to the pig's head with masking tape. Now stick two more layers of papier mâché over the pig's body, legs, nose and ears. Cut a slit in the top to drop the money through.

6. When the pig is completely dry and hard you can paint it with water colour or poster paints. Brush on a layer of white paint first and then let it dry. Decorate the pig and paint on its eyes, nostrils and a mouth.

BRIGHT BUTTONS

Make your own animal, flower, heart, and alphabet buttons out of brightly coloured self-hardening clay or painted salt-dough. You can sew them on to thick paper and turn them into really special birthday, thankyou and invitation cards, as well as unusual pictures for presents.

Things you need

Self-hardening clay in bright colours
Tracing paper and a pencil
Scissors
Thick paper or card
Felt tips pens
Sewing thread and a needle
A baking tray and a knife
Clear varnish or clear nail varnish

Design a special card for valentine's day.

Make small number buttons to sew on a cardigan.

10

Make a friend their name in letter buttons.

HANDY HINTS

If you do not have any self-hardening clay, make the buttons out of salt-dough (see page 6 for the recipe). Paint and varnish the dough buttons when you have baked them.

Instead of making a tracing paper shape to cut around, buy tiny petit-four pastry cutters in different shapes to make your buttons.

Make a special set of buttons for one of your friends to sew on her cardigan.

Froggy button picture

1. Draw a funny frog's face on a sheet of tracing paper, like this. Cut out the paper frog shape and use it as a template. Or try designing your own buttons.

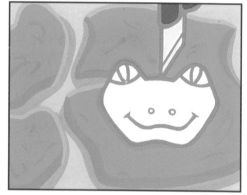

2. Roll out some green self-hardening clay, about as thick as a button. Put the frog shape on the clay and cut around it with a knife. Cut out three frog faces.

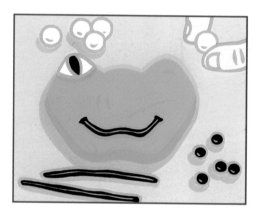

3. Roll out six little white balls of clay and six black balls for the frogs' eyes. Press them on to the three faces, as shown. Press on black mouths.

4. Make two holes in the middle of each face with a needle. Then put the buttons on a baking tray. Bake them in the oven until they are completely hard.

5. Take the buttons out of the oven and let them cool. Then paint a layer of varnish on the front of each button. When they are dry, varnish the backs.

6. Fold some stiff paper or card in half. Sew the frog buttons on to the card and draw a picture around them with felt tips, such as some lily pads.

PASTA PRESENTS

Brightly painted pasta shapes can be turned into magnificent jewellery very easily. They also make pretty decorations around photograph frames or on a mirror. Try making this pasta bow jewellery box and filling it will pasta jewels.

Things you need

Different pasta shapes - bows,
  spirals, shells, wheels or animals
A cardboard box
Poster paints (including gold)
Paintbrushes
Water-based varnish or nail varnish
Thin ribbon or rolled elastic
Scissors and strong glue,
  such as UHU

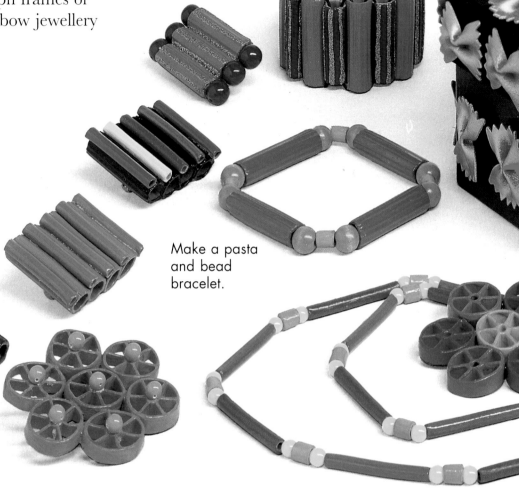

Make a pasta and bead bracelet.

Perfect pasta brooches

Pasta bow box

1. Before you start gluing them on, arrange the pasta bows on the top and sides of the cardboard box to see how they will look and how many you need.

2. Spread glue over the box, a little at a time. Then stick the pasta bows on to the glue. Do this until you have covered the top and sides of the box.

3. When all the bows are stuck firmly on to the box, paint them with gold poster paint. When the paint is dry, paint the bows with clear water-based varnish.

Pasta bow
jewellery box

HANDY HINTS

If you do not have a plain coloured box, you can paint it before you start gluing on the pasta.

Always varnish your pasta jewellery after you have painted it. Otherwise it might get soggy if it gets wet or damp.

To make pasta jewellery look very rich, paint it with gold or silver paint, cover it with glue and dip it in glitter. You can also use glitter glue.

Pretty
pasta tube
necklace

Pretty pasta necklace

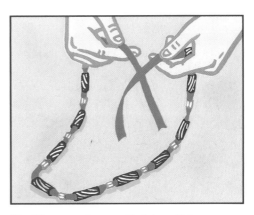

1. Paint some long and short spiral pasta tubes with brightly coloured poster paints. It is best to paint the tubes half at a time and then let them dry.

2. When the paint is absolutely dry, carefully brush a thick layer of clear nail varnish over each one of the pasta tubes. Leave the varnish to dry completely.

3. Cut a piece of thin ribbon a little longer than you want the necklace to be. Then thread the painted pasta on to the ribbon and tie the ends in a bow.

13

PAINTED PLATES

These painted plates make wonderful presents to hang on the wall. You can paint them with bright patterns or pictures, for Christmas, birthdays or for a new baby. It is best to use glazed china plates and special enamel paints or acrylic paints. You can buy them from most good craft shops or model shops.

Things you need

Paper, a pencil and coloured pens
A white glazed china plate
A chinagraph pencil
Paintbrushes and white spirit
Enamel or acrylic paints in
 bright colours
Saucers to mix colours

Hang your
breakfast plate
in the kitchen.

Paint a
clown plate
for a baby.

Paint a pattern
instead of a
picture.

Sausages, eggs and chips

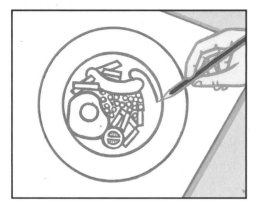

1. Draw around your plate on to some paper. Then draw and colour a fried egg, two sausages, a tomato, chips and peas on the circle of paper, like this.

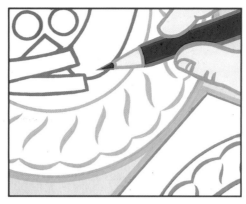

2. Turn the picture around to make sure it looks good from all angles. Then copy your design on to a plain glazed plate, using a chinagraph pencil.

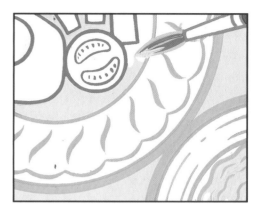

3. If you are using enamel paints, stir each colour well before you begin to paint. Do not mix your colours. Start by painting in a background colour, like this.

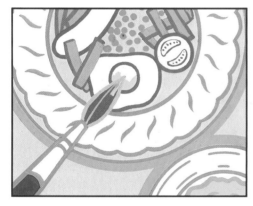

4. When the background colour is completely dry, paint in the rest of your design. Do not put too much paint on the brush but gradually build up the colour.

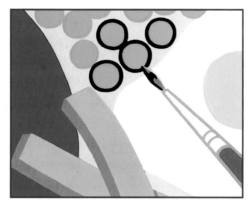

5. When you have finished painting, put the plate on some newspaper to dry completely. Then using a thin brush, add a black outline to your picture.

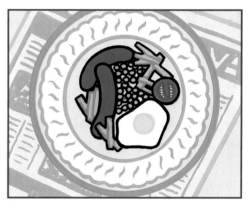

6. You will have to be very careful and keep a steady hand when you outline your picture. You can outline it in any colour or not at all if you prefer.

HANDY HINTS

Read the instructions carefully before you use your paints as different makes of enamel paint dry in different ways.

Never put your painted plates in the dishwasher as the hot water may make them peel. Wash them with washing-up liquid.

Make sure you have lots of white spirit for washing your brushes and thinning your paint. You can wipe off your mistakes with a soft cloth dipped in white spirit.

Try using acrylic paints. They are not as glossy as enamels but they dry more quickly.

FABULOUS FRAMES

Everybody loves being given photographs of their family, friends or pets, especially if they are nicely framed. Try making these fabulous frames out of cardboard decorated with metal or tin foil. You can also make shiny foil Christmas decorations and candle holders.

Things you need

Paper, a pencil and ruler
Cardboard, scissors and masking tape
Metal foil from an empty tomato
  paste tube, or tin foil cut from an
  unused foil baking tray
A photograph
A ball point pen
Strong glue or a glue stick

Tomato paste
tube frame

Shiny Christmas
tree decorations

Tin foil frame

16

Design your own candle holders.

Heart frame

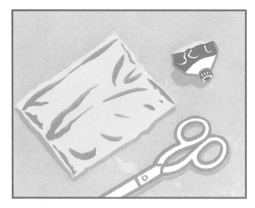

1. Cut the lid off an empty tomato paste tube with some scissors. Cut the tube open and wash it out. Then flatten it by rubbing your thumb hard over the bumps. Let the metal foil dry.

2. Draw a heart shape, about 13 cm high, on some cardboard. It should be no bigger than your piece of foil. Draw a rectangle, about 10 cm long and 3 cm wide. Cut out both cardboard shapes.

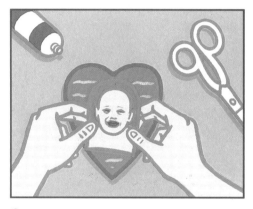

3. Cut out the photograph you want to frame and glue it to the middle of the cardboard heart, like this. It is probably best to cut out just the face so it will show through the frame.

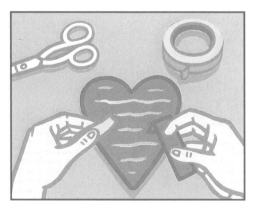

4. Using the tips of your scissors, score a line across the rectangular cardboard shape, about 2 cm from one end. Fold it over and tape it to the back of the heart shape with masking tape.

5. Draw around the cardboard heart shape on to the written side of the metal foil with a ball point pen. Cut it out. Then draw a smaller heart in the middle of the foil, like this, and cut it out.

6. Using a ball point pen, draw patterns on the back of the foil heart. Press quite hard. Then stick the heart, shiny side up, on to the cardboard heart, with the photograph showing through.

MERRY MOBILES

Colourful mobiles make very good presents for babies because they love to look at interesting things that move about. Try choosing a theme, such as animals, monsters or these birds, when you are designing your mobile. Make the colours bright and the shapes very simple.

Things you need

Paper and a pencil
10 squares of felt in
  bright colours
A needle and some
  strong thread
Fabric glue, such as Copydex
A pair of scissors and
  some pins
A lampshade ring or
  wooden embroidery ring
Coloured thread
  or wool

Make the birds as colourful as possible.

Bright bird mobile

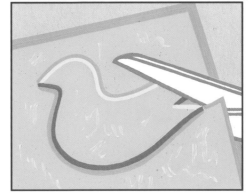

1. Draw a simple bird shape, like this, on some thin cardboard. Cut it out. Put the card shape on a felt square and draw around it. Cut out a felt bird.

2. Glue the felt bird on to the same coloured felt square and cut around it so you have a double thick felt bird. Make ten birds, each in a different coloured felt.

3. Now draw a wing shape, like this, on some thin cardboard. Cut it out. Put it on some felt and cut around it. Cut out ten pairs of wings in different colours.

HANDY HINTS

You can make the felt animals with or without wadding in the middle. The wadding makes them a little bit thicker and stiffer.

Instead of sticking the felt shapes together, try sewing them together with bright thread.

Look in children's books to get ideas for your mobile and for simple shapes to copy.

Magic moons
and stars mobile

Monster
mobile

4. Stick a wing on to each side of every felt bird. Then cut out 20 round felt eyes and 20 coloured beaks. Stick them on to both sides of each bird. Let the glue dry.

5. Sew a long piece of coloured thread with a knot in one end to the middle of each bird, like this. Tie the birds at different lengths around the lampshade ring.

6. Tie three pieces of coloured thread, about 30 cm long, around the ring. Knot the ends together. Hang up the mobile and move the birds along until it balances.

19

BRILLIANT BEADS

On these two pages you can find out how to make all sorts of beads from self-hardening clay. Most craft shops and department stores sell it in bright colours. Try making your own designs and shapes. You can mix colours together to make exciting and interesting patterns.

Things you need

Self-hardening clay in bright colours
Kitchen foil and a toothpick
Thin coloured string or ribbon

Flower and bead
necklace

Big bright necklace

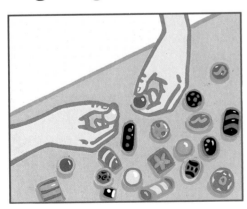

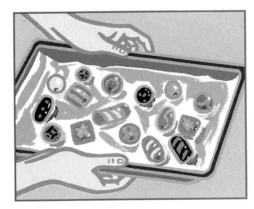

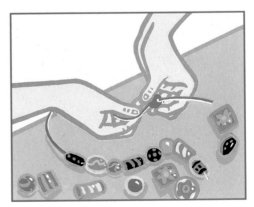

1. Choose the big bright beads you want to make or design beads of your own. Try making them in lots of different sizes, colours and patterns.

2. Push a toothpick through each bead to make a hole so you can thread them. Put the beads on foil on a baking tray. Bake them in the oven until they are hard.

3. When the beads are cool, decide which ones you want to put next to each other to make a necklace or bracelet. Thread the beads on to some coloured string.

HANDY HINTS

It is easier to mould self-hardening clay once you have softened it in your hands. Roll it out on to a clean surface to stop it getting dirty, and make sure that you keep the colours separate.

It helps to draw the design of your beads on some paper before you start to make them, and to choose which colours you want to use.

You can varnish your beads once they are baked to make them more colourful and shiny.

Roll out long, thin strips of clay to decorate different shapes, like these fish and the wheels.

Big bright beads

To make this bead, roll out very thin strips of clay and some tiny balls. Press them on to a square bead to make a face.

To make a flower, flatten a small ball of clay. Cut out six wedges with a knife. Then mould the petals with your fingers.

To make a stripy bead, make two separate beads in different colours. Slice the beads and then put them together, first one colour and then the other. Roll until it is smooth.

To make this flower, press five little triangles of clay on to a flat bead in a flower shape. Very carefully flatten the flower with a rolling pin. Add the centre and the stripes.

For a marbled bead, mix two colours together in a ball. Roll the ball until it is completely smooth.

For this bead, make a big, round white bead. Flatten out a small red ball and a small white ball. Roll them up together like a Swiss roll. Cut thin slices off the roll. Press them on to the big bead and roll.

21

FUNNY FAMILY MODELS

For a really original present, try making funny models of your family and friends, and even your pets, that look just like them. You can make them out of salt-dough (see page 6 for the recipe). The models look even funnier if you give each person a special feature that reminds you especially of them.

Things you need

Salt-dough (see page 6)
Water colour or poster paints
Paintbrushes
Clear varnish or nail varnish
A garlic press
A toothpick for making
  holes
A pencil and a knife
A baking tray

Make an angel as a Christmas decoration.

Make a nice fat Santa Claus.

Model of mum

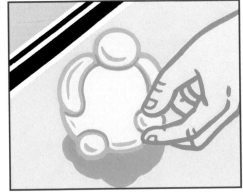

1. Draw a picture of the person you want to model, or use a photograph. The model must have a solid body, like this, to stand on when it is baked.

2. Roll a big ball of dough for the body and press it on to a baking tray. Press on a smaller ball for the head. Make sausage shaped arms and little round feet.

3. When you have made the body, add the person's features. Push balls of dough through a garlic press for the hair. Press on a little round nose and a mouth.

Make a whole family of salt-dough models.

HANDY HINTS

Salt-dough models take different lengths of time to bake hard in the oven depending on how big and fat they are. It is best to check them while they are cooking. Small figures take about 30 to 40 minutes.

Knead the dough well before you use it. The softer it is, the easier it is to use.

It is best to make your models small and fat rather than too tall as they spread out when they are baking.

4. Use a toothpick to poke holes for the eyes and to make finger lines. Now add something special that reminds you of the person, such as a particular dress or tie.

5. Let the model dry out a little. Then put it in the oven at 180°C until it is hard. Take it out and let it cool. Paint it with bright poster paints or water colours.

6. When the paint is dry, varnish the model all over and leave it to dry. Then brush another coat of varnish on to the front and back. Leave it to dry.

MARVELLOUS MAGNETS

These colourful magnets are easy and fun to make and are very good presents for people of all ages. They stick on to any metal surface, such as a fridge, or a filing cabinet and are useful for holding up notes, lists and pictures.

Things you need
for jelly bean magnets

Brightly coloured jelly beans
Small, round magnets (available from
  toy shops and hardware stores)
Small sweet paper cases and strong glue
Clear water-based varnish and a paintbrush

Other things to use

Small colourful objects make the best and prettiest magnets. You will probably be able to find lots of good things to use around the house. This list gives you an idea of some of the things to use. Most just need a magnet stuck on the back, but some may need to be varnished.

Sweets, such as jelly beans and marzipan
  fruits stuck into small paper sweet holders
Fruit lollipops
Small boxes, such as raisin boxes, soap boxes,
  used matchboxes and sweet boxes
Small biscuits or crackers

HANDY HINTS

Allow lots of time for the coats of varnish to dry on your magnets. Start making them a few days before you want to give them away as presents.

If you are using biscuits or sweets, it is best to let them dry out before you varnish them.

Before you start, varnish one of the sweets to test that the colour does not run.

Pretty parcel magnets

Bright bow magnet

Magnets made from modelling clay

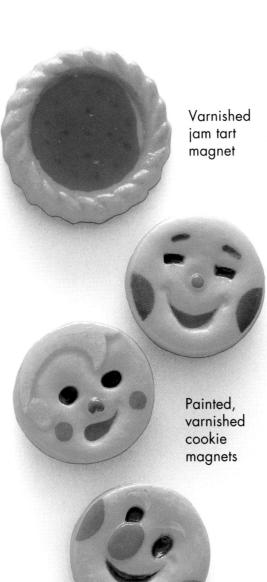

Varnished
jam tart
magnet

Use lots of
different
kinds of
sweets.

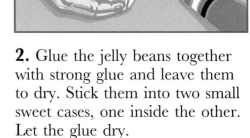

Painted,
varnished
cookie
magnets

A basketful of
flowers

Jelly bean magnet

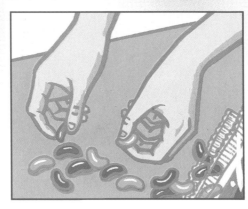

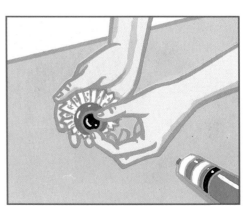

1. Arrange some jelly beans in a sweet paper case to see how many you need. Make sure they are not too heavy for the size magnet you are going to use.

2. Glue the jelly beans together with strong glue and leave them to dry. Stick them into two small sweet cases, one inside the other. Let the glue dry.

3. Cover the sweets and cases in clear varnish. Let them dry and then varnish them again three or four times. Make sure the varnish dries between each coat.

4. As soon as the varnish is dry and hard, stick a magnet on to the bottom of the paper sweet case. Let it dry. Now try making other kinds of magnets.

25

FELT PICTURES

These fantastic felt pictures make perfect presents for mums, dads and grandparents. They are made out of pieces of brightly coloured felt stuck or sewn on top of each other. They can also be decorated with buttons, beads and colourful embroidery thread. If you do not have any felt, you can use another kind of fabric instead.

Things you need

A sheet of drawing paper
Some tracing paper
A pencil and a rubber
Scissors
Fabric glue, such as Copydex
Different brightly coloured
  squares of felt
Dressmaker's pins

My Dad

Cool cat picture

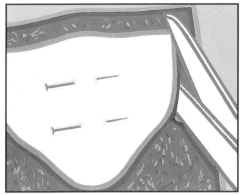

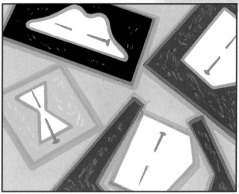

1. On a sheet of paper, draw the picture you are going to make the same size as you want it to be. Start with something simple, such as this cool cat.

2. Trace the cat's face on to some tracing paper and cut it out. Use this as a paper pattern. Pin the paper pattern on to a square of felt and cut around it.

3. Now trace around the cat's hat, bow tie, shirt and coat. Cut them out separately. Pin each paper pattern on to a different coloured felt square and cut them out.

26

Cool cat

My house

4. Using fabric glue, stick the felt cat's face on to a big square of felt of a different colour. Then glue on the hat, bow tie, shirt and coat, like this. Let the glue dry.

5. Cut out and glue some long whiskers on to the cat's cheeks. Trace and cut out some sunglasses and glue them on to the cat's face. Glue a band on the hat.

6. Cut out some small pieces of felt for the nose, mouth and ears and glue them on. Add different coloured lapels and a pocket handkerchief to the coat.

BEAUTIFUL BOWS

These beautiful bows are very easy to make from just newspaper, glue and paint. They can be made into brooches and earrings, or turned into colourful cuff links. Decorated with poster paints and then varnished, they can be stuck on to hair bands or hair combs and on to shoes.

Things you need

Newspaper
Wallpaper paste or PVA glue
  mixed with water
A bowl of water
Poster paints and a paintbrush
Clear water-based varnish
  or nail varnish
Strong glue (for sticking
  on to brooch backs,
  earrings, cuff links or
  hair combs)
A brooch back

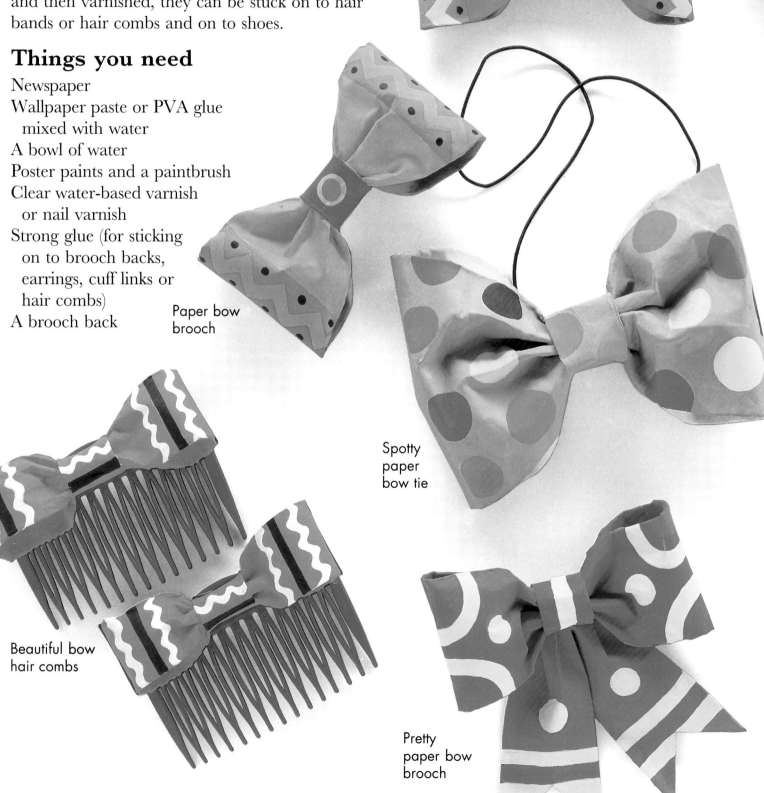

Paper bow
brooch

Spotty
paper
bow tie

Beautiful bow
hair combs

Pretty
paper bow
brooch

Snappy
shoe bows

HANDY HINTS

If you stick several layers of paper together at the same time, they will take longer to dry, but the papier mâché will be much stronger.

Remember to decide what size to make the bow before you start. Big bows are best for bow ties and brooches, medium-sized ones look good on hair bands or hair combs. Smaller bows make pretty earrings, cuff links and shoe bows.

Paper bow brooch

1. Mix up the wallpaper paste following the instructions on the packet. Then rip up large sheets of newspaper into quarters and soak them, one by one, in cold water, for a few seconds.

2. Take the paper out of the water and lie it flat on a table. Peel off the top strip and spread glue over it with your hands or a paintbrush. Carefully rip the glued paper in half lengthways.

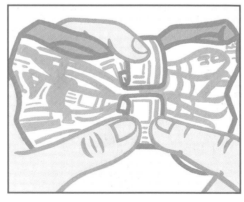

3. Stick one half of the paper to the other so that an unglued side sticks to a glued one. Do this again so you have a long strip of paper four layers deep. Cut off a strip at one end.

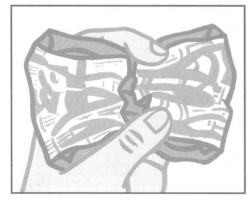

4. Fold in the edges of the long strip to neaten them. Then fold the two ends into the middle to make a bow shape, like this. Pinch the middle to make the bow look nice and full.

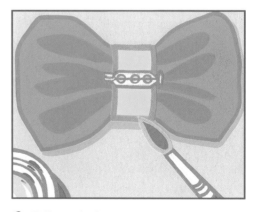

5. Now fold in the edges of the little strip to neaten them. Wrap the strip around the bow so that it covers the join in the middle. Fold the ends under. Then leave the bow to dry.

6. When it is dry, decorate the bow with poster paint. Let it dry and then paint on a pattern. Stick the bow on to a brooch back with strong glue, such as UHU. Then varnish it to make it look shiny.

PICTURE PRESENTS

Old boxes and tins can be made to look very pretty by decorating them with lots of tiny pictures or patterns cut out from postcards, glossy magazines, birthday cards or wrapping paper, and then varnished. You can also try decorating hairbrushes, hand mirrors and photograph frames with cut-out pictures.

Things you need

A box or tin
Old magazines, wrapping paper,
 birthday cards or postcards
A pair of small scissors
Strong glue or a glue stick
Clear water-based varnish
Fine sandpaper
A paintbrush
A soft cloth

Make a frame to cover with pictures.

Picture box

Cover and varnish a box for dad with old stamps.

Choose a simple picture to stick on a hairbrush.

Pretty picture box

1. Before you start, make sure that the box or tin is clean and smooth so that it is ready to decorate. Peel off any labels or bumpy bits.

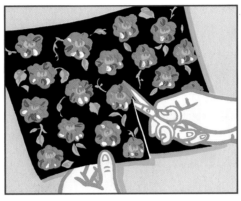

2. Using a pair of small, sharp scissors, carefully cut out the pictures you want to cover the box with. To start with, practise cutting out bigger pictures.

3. Arrange the pictures on the box and then glue on the first one. Rub hard to get rid of any air bubbles and to make a nice smooth surface.

4. Wipe off any extra glue with a soft cloth and then glue on the next picture. Carry on until you have covered the box with little pictures. Let the glue dry.

5. Once the glue has dried you can begin to varnish. Brush on the first coat and leave it to dry overnight. Then gently sand it down with fine sandpaper.

6. Dust the box and then varnish on another coat. Let each coat dry before adding the next. You will need ten layers of varnish. Do not sand the last coat.

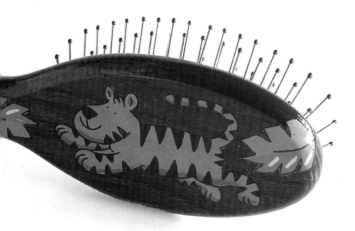

HANDY HINTS

It is best to use good quality pictures to decorate your presents. Save wrapping paper, Christmas and birthday cards, as well as postcards.

Before you start, decide what kinds of pictures you are going to use, such as birds or flowers. You can also use old stamps, sweet papers, and even shells, buttons, sequins or beads.

GLORIOUS GLOVES

Here is a really different kind of present to give to someone and make them laugh. You can buy cheap washing-up gloves and cotton gloves in lots of bright colours from hardware shops or department stores to make these crazy gloves.

Things you need
for the washing-up gloves

A pair of red rubber gloves
  and a pair of yellow ones
A colourful plastic carrier bag
A needle, thread and pins
Strong glue, such as UHU
Scissors and a pencil

For the dusting glove

A cotton glove
A pink or yellow duster or cloth
A square of red or bright
  pink felt for the nails
Some diamantés and sequins
Fabric glue or a needle
  and thread

Cut circles out of balloons to decorate the gloves.

Wild washing-up gloves

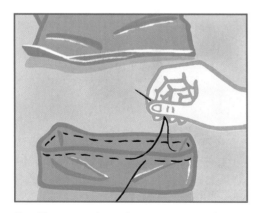

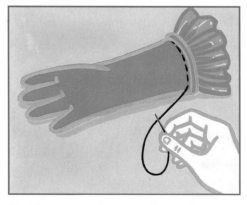

1. Cut a strip, about 8 cm wide and 40 cm long, out of a plastic carrier bag. Thread a needle and sew a running stitch as close to one edge as possible, like this.

2. Take out the needle and pull up the thread to make a frilly cuff. When it is small enough to fit around a red rubber glove, pin it and sew it on, as shown.

3. Do the same to the other red glove. Then cut out ten yellow nails and some flowers from the yellow rubber glove. Stick them on the gloves with rubber glue.

Dainty
dusting glove

Grisly
gardening
gloves

Dainty dusting glove

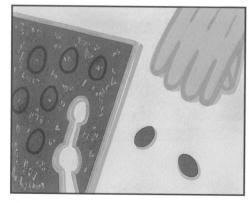

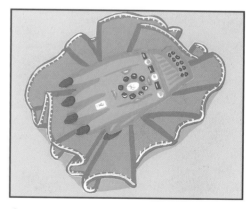

1. Draw ten fingernails on to the red felt. Make sure they are big enough to fit on to the ends of the fingers of a cotton glove. Then cut them out.

2. Using some fabric glue, stick one red felt nail on to the tip of each finger of the cotton glove, as if they were real fingernails. Leave the glue to dry.

3. Carefully stick or sew the duster to the middle of the glove, as shown. Then stick or sew bright diamantés and sequins on to the glove to decorate it.

SWEET PRESENTS

When you do not have much time to make a present, why not give some delicious home-made sweets. All these sweets are very quick to make as they do not need to be cooked. You can make them extra special by putting them in a pretty box or basket tied with a bow.

Things you need
for the marzipan fruits

125 grams icing sugar
125 grams castor sugar
225 grams ground almonds
1 beaten egg
Juice of a lemon
Different coloured food
   colourings
A bowl, wooden spoon
   and a fork

for the coconut ice

A small can of condensed milk
250 grams of icing sugar
1 teaspoon of vanilla essence
17 grams desiccated coconut
Red food colouring
2 bowls and a Swiss roll tin
A wooden spoon
   and a knife
A sieve

Fill a tiny basket with all kinds of marzipan fruit.

Put the coconut ice in paper sweet cases in a box.

34

Marzipan fruits

1. Mix the icing sugar, castor sugar and ground almonds in a bowl. Add the beaten egg. If the mixture is too dry, add lemon juice, a little at a time, until you have a soft ball of marzipan.

2. Divide the marzipan into four separate lumps. Put each lump into a bowl. Then add a few drops of a different colour food colouring to each bowl. Mix it in well with a fork.

3. Shape the marzipan mixture into fruits - red for strawberries and plums, yellow for bananas and lemons, green for apples and pears. Use cloves for stalks and green marzipan to make leaves.

Make lines on the bananas.

Dip the strawberries in sugar.

Roll the oranges around the outside of a fine grater.

Coconut ice

(image at cx 0.78 cy 0.72)

1. Sieve the sugar into a bowl and then add the vanilla essence and condensed milk. Add the desiccated coconut and stir the mixture with a wooden spoon until it becomes stiff.

2. Divide the mixture in half and put one half in the second bowl. Add a few drops of red food colouring to one of the mixtures and stir it until it becomes pale pink.

3. Put the white mixture in the bottom of the Swiss roll tin. Put it in the fridge until firm. Spread the pink mixture on top and put it in the fridge. When it is hard cut the coconut ice into squares.

GREAT GINGERBREAD PRESENTS

Gingerbread is simple to make and delicious to eat. You can make it into almost any shape you like, such as gingerbread people and animals, a gingerbread house, decorations to hang on a Christmas tree, and even name plates for your friends and family.

Things you need

250 grams self-raising flour
1 tablespoon ground ginger
75 grams butter
125 grams golden syrup
125 grams soft brown sugar
3 tablespoons milk
Plain flour (for flouring work top)
Margarine or oil (for greasing
  a baking tray)
A tube of ready-made icing
A sieve, large bowl and
  a wooden spoon
A rolling pin and a baking tray
Pastry cutters in different
  shapes and sizes

A gingerbread family

Making the gingerbread

1. Turn the oven on to 150 °C. Sieve the flour and ginger together into the bowl. Then, using your fingertips, rub the butter into the mixture.

2. Mix the syrup, sugar and milk together and add them to the flour mixture. Mix them into a dough. Put the dough in the fridge for half an hour.

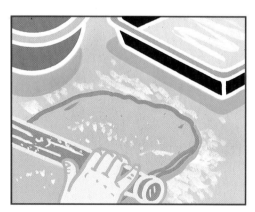

3. Grease the baking tin with oil or margarine. Lightly flour the work top and then roll out the dough with a rolling pin to a thickness of about 5 mm.

HANDY HINTS

If you do not have pastry cutters, use cardboard shapes and cut around them.

Weigh the syrup in a plastic cup. But remember to weigh the cup first.

To get syrup off a spoon, rub the spoon with butter, dip it in flour and then put the spoon in the syrup.

Gingerbread Christmas decorations

Gingerbread name plates

Gingerbread animals

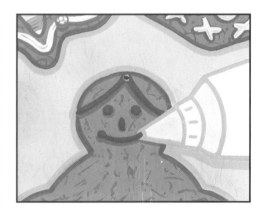

4. Using pastry cutters, cut out some gingerbread shapes. Put them on the baking tray, leaving gaps between the shapes to allow them to spread.

5. Make a small hole near the top of the each shape with a skewer. Bake the shapes in the oven for 10 to 15 minutes, or until they are golden brown.

6. When the gingerbread shapes are cool, draw faces, names or patterns on them with the icing. Thread ribbon through the holes before you give them away.

PAPER POTS

These colourful pots are made out of papier mâché. They make wonderful fruit bowls, pencil and pen holders, or special vases for flowers. You can paint your own designs on the pots or decorate them with different coloured sugar or tissue paper.

Things you need

A large bowl (to use as a mould)
Cling film or vaseline
Old newspaper
PVA glue or wallpaper paste
A bowl for mixing glue
A paintbrush and water
Poster paints
Scissors
Clear water-based varnish

Papier mâché a jam jar to make a waterproof vase. Keep the jar in place for the water.

Perfect paper pot

Perfect paper pot

1. Cover the outside of the bowl you are using as a mould with cling film. Make sure that the cling film covers the edge of the bowl. This will stop the papier mâché from sticking to the edge.

2. Mix the PVA glue with three times as much water. Then stir them together until they are mixed well. Put the glue mixture into a glass jar with a screw lid so that it will keep.

3. Tear the newspaper into big pieces. Drop them, one by one, into 10 cm of water in a sink. Wet them for five minutes and then carefully take them out. Lay them down on a work surface.

38

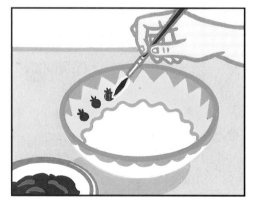

 To make a pencil holder, papier mâché an old salt tin or box. Separate it from the cling film with a knife.

HANDY HINTS

Instead of using cling film, you can use vaseline to stop the papier mâché sticking to the bowl.

If the papier mâché shell tears when you take it off the bowl, mend it with masking tape. Papier mâché over the tear.

You can use wallpaper paste (see pages 8-9) instead of PVA glue mixed with water. But the PVA dries faster.

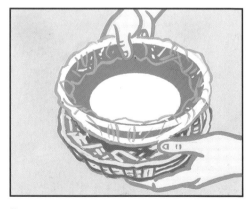

4. Tear the wet newspaper into small strips. Cover the bowl with a layer of strips. Make sure that they overlap so that they cover the cling film. Brush the PVA glue mixture over the strips.

5. Cover the glue with more strips. Let it dry. Add more glue and paper until you have five or six layers of papier mâché. When it is dry, separate the paper and glue shell from the bowl.

6. Trim the edges with scissors. Paint the bowl all over with white poster paint. When it is dry, paint on bright patterns. To give it a glossy look, brush on a layer of the glue mixture or varnish.

COLOURFUL CANDLE HOLDERS

For special occasions, such as Christmas, birthday parties or even spooky Hallowe'en parties, it is fun to have candles burning on the table. Try making these colourful salt-dough candle holders to help decorate the table.

Things you need

Ready-made salt-dough (see page 6)
A rolling pin, knife and baking tray
Round pastry cutters or a glass
Thin cardboard and scissors
Poster paints and a paintbrush
Clear water-based varnish
 or nail varnish
Strong glue and plasticine
Two thin candles

Make a green slithery snake candle holder.

Make a deep candle holder and fill it with sweets.

Make holders for thick candles.

Christmas candle holder

Spooky spider holder

40

Christmas candle holders

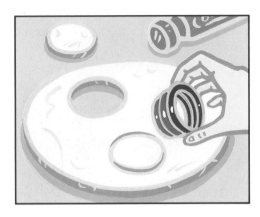

1. Turn the oven on to 180 °C. Roll out the dough until it is about 10 mm thick. Cut out two circles of dough with a round pastry cutter or a wine glass.

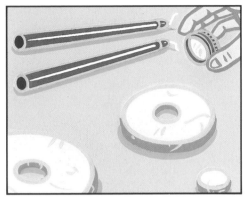

2. Cut out a circle in the middle of the round shapes of dough, a little bigger than the end of a candle. Use a small round pastry cutter or a bottle top.

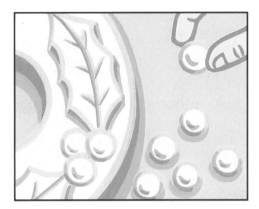

3. Cut out salt-dough holly leaves with a knife and roll small balls to make the berries. Stick them around the circle of dough with water, as shown.

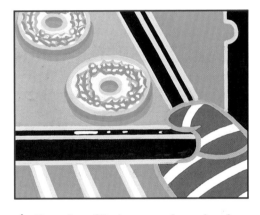

4. Put the Christmas rings in the oven on a baking tray until they are hard. This should take about 1½ hours. Take them out and let them cool completely.

5. When they are cool, put the rings on a piece of cardboard and draw around them. Cut out the card circles. Stick them on to the bottom of the rings, like this.

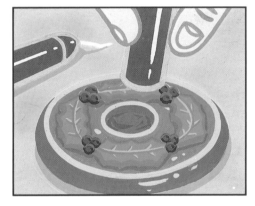

6. Paint the candle holders with poster paints. When the paint is dry, brush on a layer of varnish. Stick plasticine in the holes and press in the candles.

HANDY HINTS

Let the salt-dough candle holders dry out a little before you bake them in the oven.

Instead of using pastry cutters, you can cut out the dough rings with tin lids or ramekin dishes.

You can make little bowls for your candles by covering an upturned ramekin dish with salt-dough and baking it in the oven. Be very careful not to break the salt-dough shell when you take it off the ramekin dish.

POT PLANT STICKS

For a really unusual present, especially for people who love flowers and gardening, you can make these pot plant sticks. They are very useful for propping up flowers in a pot plant and they also help to drain the water through the soil.

Things you need

Thin wooden sticks about 20 cm long
  (thin dowelling rods, garden canes or
  kebab sticks are best)
Scraps of brightly coloured felt
Self-hardening clay in bright colours
Fabric glue and a baking tray
A pencil and paper

Spooky
glow-in-the-dark
skull stick

Felt flower
plant sticks

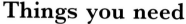

Modelling
clay fish
stick

Two-faced
pig stick

Use glow-in-the-
dark modelling
clay to make this
spooky spider.

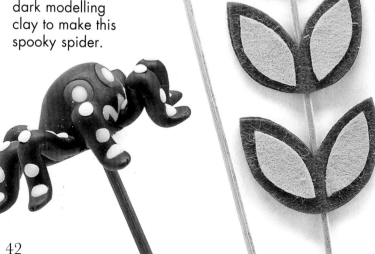

42

HANDY HINTS

Use old lollipop sticks or ice cream sticks to make plant sticks for tiny pots. They also make good table decorations for parties.

Try making some spooky plant sticks with special glow-in-the-dark clay.

Painted salt-dough (see page 6), papier mâché animals, flowers, bows and thick painted card shapes make good pot plant sticks.

Felt flower plant stick

 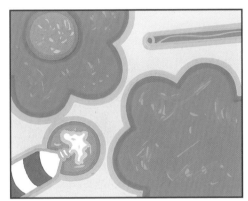 

1. Draw a flower on some paper and cut it out. Pin the shape on some felt and cut around it. Do this again. Cut out two felt leaves and two flower centres.

2. Spread glue on to one side of each of the flower centres and stick them on to the middle of the flower shapes, like this. Leave the glue to dry completely.

3. Glue the flowers together, as shown, with the top of the stick sandwiched between them. Stick the leaves together with the stick between one end.

Two-faced pig stick

 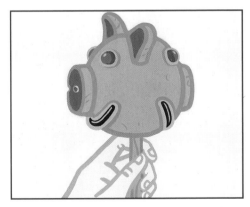 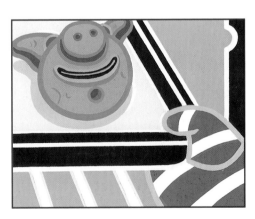

1. Roll a ball of bright pink self-hardening clay for the pig's head and two smaller balls for it's noses Make four little blue eyes, two pink ears and two black mouths.

2. Press a nose, two eyes and a mouth on to each side of the head. Put on the ears. Push a stick into the head where the neck would be, about 3 cm deep.

3. Take the stick out and bake the pig's head in the oven at about 130 °C until it is hard. Before the clay cools, push the stick back into the hole.

CRAZY STRING HOLDERS

Turn your empty yoghurt pots or plastic cartons
into these crazy animal heads. Fixed to the wall,
they make brilliant holders for string, ribbon and
wool. You can use all sorts of different shaped
and sized pots which you can probably find
around the house.

Things you need

Empty plastic cartons
Thin cardboard (an old cereal
   packet is ideal)
Acrylic paints and a paintbrush
A pencil
Scissors and drawing pins
Small balls of string, ribbon
   or wool
Strong glue or a glue stick
Beads for the tiger's eyes

Stripy tiger
string holder

Stripy tiger holder

1. Wash out an empty yoghurt
pot or carton. Soak it in water
and peel off any labels. When it
is dry, draw around the pot on to
some thin cardboard, like this.

2. For the stripy tiger, add big
round ears. Carefully cut around
them and the cardboard shape.
Then cut a flap, like this, in the
middle of the cardboard shape.

3. Cover the pot with a thick
layer of white acrylic paint. Let it
dry. Then paint on a layer of
orange paint and let it dry. Paint
on the tiger's stripes, as shown.

Big bull holder

HANDY HINTS

Do not put a big ball of string or wool into your crazy string holder. Otherwise it may be too heavy and pull the holder off the wall.

You can stick all sorts of things on to your string heads to make them look even crazier. Use cotton wool for sheep, wool for a horse's mane, buttons for noses and beads for eyes.

Porky pig holder

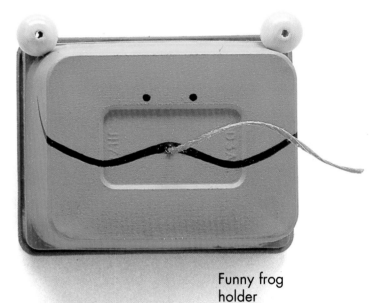

Funny frog holder

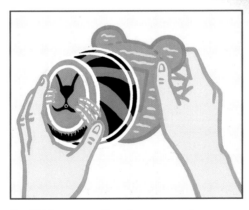

4. When the paint is dry, paint on the tiger's nose and mouth. Make sure the mouth is where you want the string to come out. Glue on some string whiskers.

5. Using small scissors, poke a hole in the mouth. Then glue the cardboard shape you have cut out on to the back of the pot. Paint the tiger's ears orange and black.

6. Glue on bead eyes. Put some string into the pot. Pull one end through the tiger's mouth. To stick the holder on the wall, push a drawing pin through each ear.

WRAPPING IT UP

Now that you have made your presents, it is very important to know how to wrap them up properly to make them look extra special. Here are some good wrapping-up ideas and ways to decorate your presents with bows and paper ribbons. Instead of buying paper you could try and make your own.

Things you need

Wrapping paper
Invisible sticky tape
Scissors
A ball of thin paper ribbon
Sheets of paper in lots of
    different colours

Use a potato or stencil to print patterns on your home-made wrapping paper.

You can make long, tricky-shaped presents look like real crackers. Tie bows around the ends.

46

The perfect present

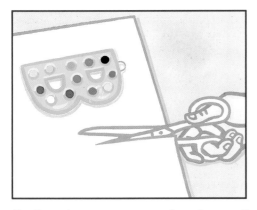

1. Put the present on the sheet of wrapping paper to see how much you need. Make sure you have enough to fold in both ends and to overlap the paper at the top. Cut the paper.

2. Put the present face-down on the paper. Fold the long edges over the top so that they overlap. Make sure the paper is tight before you stick it down with invisible sticky tape.

3. Turn one end of the present towards you and fold in the ends as neatly as possible to make corner folds, as shown. Stick them down. Do the same to the other end of the paper.

Curls and bows

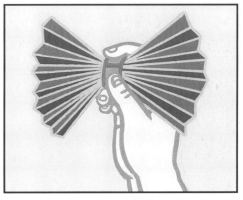

1. Decorate your present with curly paper ribbon. To make it curl, hold the ribbon between your thumb and the blade of some scissors. Then firmly pull the blade along the ribbon.

2. You can make your own paper curls by cutting out strips of paper and wrapping them around a wooden spoon or stick. Try making them in different widths and different colours.

3. Make a pleated paper bow by folding some paper over and over again, like a concertina. Pinch the middle together and wrap a strip of paper around it. Stick it with sticky tape or glue.

Make gift tags out of coloured paper. Tie them on with thin ribbon

HANDY HINTS

To make your parcels look really neat, fold in the sides and ends of your paper before you start to wrap them up.

If you do not have any wrapping paper you can use left-over rolls of wallpaper or kitchen tin foil. You can also decorate plain paper with potato prints or stencils.

48

PRINTED IN BELGIUM BY

INTERNATIONAL BOOK PRODUCTION